A GENEROUS LATITUDE

LENEA GRACE

ECW

Published by ECW Press
665 Gerrard Street East, Toronto, ON M4M 1Y2 | 416-694-3348 | info@ecwpress.com

MISFIT

Editor for the press: Michael Holmes
Cover design: David A. Gee
Author photo: Alexa Garrey
Type: Rachel Ironstone

Library and Archives Canada Cataloguing in Publication
Grace, Lenea, author | A generous latitude : poems / Lenea Grace.
Issued in print and electronic formats.
ISBN 978-1-77041-421-1 (softcover); ISBN 978-1-77305-189-5 (PDF); ISBN 978-1-77305-188-8 (epub)
I. Title.
PS8613.R3327G46 2018 C811'.6 C2017-906208-5 | C2017-906209-3

The publication of *A Generous Latitude* has been generously supported by the Canada Council for the Arts, which last year invested $153 million to bring the arts to Canadians throughout the country, and by the Government of Canada through the Canada Book Fund. *Nous remercions le Conseil des arts du Canada de son soutien. L'an dernier, le Conseil a investi 153 millions de dollars pour mettre de l'art dans la vie des Canadiennes et des Canadiens de tout le pays. Ce livre est financé en partie par le gouvernement du Canada.* We also acknowledge the support of the Ontario Arts Council (OAC), an agency of the Government of Ontario, which last year funded 1,737 individual artists and 1,095 organizations in 223 communities across Ontario for a total of $52.1 million, and the contribution of the Government of Ontario through the Ontario Book Publishing Tax Credit and the Ontario Media Development Corporation.

Canada Council for the Arts | Conseil des Arts du Canada | Canada

Ontario | Ontario Media Development Corporation

ONTARIO ARTS COUNCIL
CONSEIL DES ARTS DE L'ONTARIO
an Ontario government agency
un organisme du gouvernement de l'Ontario

Printed and bound in Canada by: Coach House 5 4 3 2 1

For Pamela and Andrew

CONTENTS

Proofs 11
Pressure Drop 13
Faceblue 15
The Cock-n-Bull 17
Boat Song 18
Our Landscape 20
Door Frame, Late Morning 21
Flat Tire in Vermilion Bay 22
To Pogamasing 24
The Brash Tides 25
Tracing One Warm Line 26
Calgary, 1981 28
Hitchhikers 29
Larry Bird Mows the Lawn 31
Montreal Poem; or, Our Hearts Are Not Like Wheels; or, Les Habitants 32
Rib 34
Mercy Fuck 35
John Island I 36
TUЯBO 38
A Man I Never Loved 40
The Why and the How 42
Geography 43
John Island II 44
On Yonge Street 46
Highway 17 47
Auld Lang Syne, etc. 49
Eulogy 51

In Sechelt 52
Yukon River 53
Mr. Peanut 55
Sharp Flesh 57
Taxidermy 58
Organ Donor 60
I Remember the Words 61
Carpentry 63
Sudbury, Ont. 64
Grace Escapes 65
Germans Love David Hasselhoff 67
Blond Satan 68
Bound 69
Ice Pick Lobotomy 70
Because 71
Barber 72
Wisdom Teeth 73
Bride and Wolf 74
Orca Fart 75
Conductor 76
Just Grit 77
The Free 78
On the Derby Day 79
The Load Out/Stay 81
For Boris 82
Influence 83

Acknowledgements 85

A GENEROUS LATITUDE

PROOFS

Poutine is a Québec delicacy.
Poutine contains gravy, fries, and cheese curds.
Therefore, gravy, fries, and cheese curds are Québec delicacies.

Guy Lafleur never wore a helmet.
Guy Lafleur released a record album of hockey tips set to disco.
Therefore, there may or may not be a correlation between head injury and disco.

Margaret Trudeau hustled and bumped at Studio 54.
Margaret Trudeau was bipolar.
Therefore, she set the trend for Canada's love-hate relationship with her husband, non?

Oui, avec 24 Coupes Stanley, les Canadiens sont l'équipe la plus titrée de toute l'histoire de la LNH.
Oui, avec seulement quatre sieges dans la Chambre des communes, le Bloc Québécois est mort.
Donc, le rêve de séparatisme fond sous nos pieds.

Leonard Cohen is from Montréal.
Leonard Cohen is not French.
Therefore, Leonard Cohen is a Jew.

We pride ourselves on ars mosaica.
We pride ourselves on separate but equal.
Therefore, we are soon to be regret.

Our apologies melt into ore, kiss arse.
Our apologies span 54°40'.
Therefore, our sorries border on Pacific Rim jobs.

We're not British blue collar, but our great-grandparents were.
We're not American white trash, but we like Fort Lauderdale.
Therefore, we are unnatural shades of leather and cream.

Alberta's got beef with Ontario.
Ontario's got beef with Alberta.
Therefore, they should just do it already and get it over with.

In this Canada, we are not together.
In this Canada, we are separated by 8,030 kilometres.
Therefore, you are Vancouver and I am St. John's.
And I am the harbour, the lighthouse.
And you are the country after dark.

PRESSURE DROP

Take a glass milk bottle
and drop a lit match down
the windowed shaft.
Take a hardboiled man,
peel him, and balance
him upon the mouth-
piece.

His pelvis will meet
the opening, torso
and limbs shoot
east and west. Tap
his left foot and he will spin,
smouldered rod and flesh
and glass.

He is no weathervane,
caught unawares by the high
pressure system that circles wrists,
grazes buttocks and spine.
No match for the match,
burnt and low, feverish.

You cannot adjust
these temperatures, outside
and inside. You cannot stop
reverse ignition. You will not
tell him to jump. You will
not watch. When it happens,
you will not watch.

And it will happen.
The bottle will strangle
his size, distort
his body: a muscled parabola,
sucking down and down,

snapping vertebrae, folding,
palms touching palms,

necks, and shoulders.
Shoulders and necks
and shoulders will catch
the necks and the necks
will catch the shoulders.
Pop and release.

FACEBLUE

Your friendship means
a lot to me — no, really,
I want to thank you

for sharing your daughter's
first bowel movement.
The video was inspired.

Twelve "likes"!
Not as many as you'd hoped,
but enough to justify

another album of your cats.
I'm sorry to hear that Chairman Meow
has piles — those vet bills

must add up. There's a Kick-
starter campaign for that, you know.
Feline anal glands are no joke.

Too soon? Not soon enough?
You tell me. Your moral compass
seems to point true north —

your jaunt to Iceland exposed
me to a whole new way of life —
self-portraiture and hashtags.

#Hans
#5Krun
#grateful

Without you how could I dress myself
up for Halloween — my closet
of war bonnets and black pancake

makeup now sits stale. Without
your guidance, I would not know
what to eat for breakfast,

for lunch or dinner. Here
we are always pontificating
on eggs benny

slathered in hollandaise,
warm and yellow and smug.
Food paparazzi, cease

and desist. Where
do you find the time
for all these half-marathons

and vegan pizza parties?
When did it become kosher
to use vegan and pizza

in the same sentence?
Tell me about Israel.
Tell me about Palestine.

Tell me how to react
in 140 characters or less,
please. Thank you

for your prayers,
your precious time —
I know you have to check

in somewhere soon
and the farmers' market
closes in 15 minutes.

THE COCK-N-BULL

They used to serve us
Chinese food — remember that
Halloween spent on wontons and pints?
We sat at the bar,
bought cigarettes from the rusted
machine, the yellowed light
of Benson & Hedges
packaging illuminated
and quaint — the relics
of expo67's summer romance
with *la belle province.*
Our dalliances are not so simple,
though our French certainly is, but
General Tso's is the same in both
official languages.
See, we're communicating now
or at least I am, James.
I'm telling you to order duck sauce.
I'm telling you to give me time.

BOAT SONG

Steady as she goes, gents —
the old girl's stuffed to the gills
with canvas packs, the leathered
straps hold in our weekend

cargo — down sleeping bags
and neon swim trunks, flats
of water buried beneath
no-name cheesies,
assorted barbecue meats

thawing under LaCloche
sun — summer's gold
suffers perennial
eye-twitch, blinking
in, blinking out

from behind cliffs
and we glide heavy
over skinny water —
the poor man's fjord —
brimming with talk

fuelled by Carling Black Label
or maybe gas fumes.
When she breaks,
we are in sight of camp
(cottage is a dirty word)

red pine walls, the screened
porch facing west — long lazy
legs and threadworn T-shirts
spread out on rock
ahead. You will stand,

crane forth, one arm
waving in air thick
with honeyed stereo
surround sound —
even from this distance

Van Morrison's drift would
stone you, *oh the water, oh the water,*
flip you ass-over-teakettle
straight into the mystic.

OUR LANDSCAPE

This body, I bear.
This body, we break: lose sleep,
succumb to fevers so grandiose
we are but wayfarers.
Sing with me, David.
Bundle me in your verse and your Nordic ski socks:
fashion me a papoose: flannel
and blueberry stems, frozen.
Then put me inside.
Skate me to Long Lake.
Now stop: my fever is flaxen,
bleeding. This is a honey-blood
seeping through skin and Gore-Tex to
make a new topography.

There is no thing between us.

DOOR FRAME, LATE MORNING

Between tiles and faucets, here they are.
Here they are and he is all wild hair,
river. She has his razor in hand,
and he her knee, in the other a harmonica.
A note for every stroke of the blade.
Already he can feel the river disappear,
glints of rapids, floating naps
swept away with the lost
current. But this is current,
and this is why he will let her shave him,
why he will blow her torch songs metal
kisses that will make her laugh,
throw back her hair,
engrave his neck with miniature scars
to preserve the current.
Oh when the saints go marching in
Oh when the saints go marching in

FLAT TIRE IN VERMILION BAY

Our trunk has sprawl,
months of bulk now littered
among cigarette butts
on this gas station lawn —
hiking boots and trash mags,
tent poles and dollar store
beach mats, the scrolls

of summer migrations,
flights of young drivers
heading west, boy,
exchanging asphalt
for grit, steel-eyed
bridges — the scent
of altitude

lingers in our igloo
cooler, the busted
miracle cooler:
stolen twice and returned
by the Mounties.
HAVE YOU SEEN OUR DR. PEPPER COOLER?
The sign worked.

You emerge with cream sodas,
a homemade pepperette,
butter tarts with raisins.
We eat and survey
our mess, read a Harlequin
out loud: *The Bride Wore Boots.*

And we wear cowboy hats,
our backs pressing against
black trunks of cemented
flesh. The legs of a highway
landmark — this iron sasquatch,
slack jawed, arms outstretched,
the whites of his eyes
searing August —

TO POGAMASING

We don't sit coach
in the Budd car. No,
we ride with the baggage,
with the men in plaid
and the moose, dead. Drunk
by 10 a.m., this train rolls north,

charging through Thomson's
boreal muse, tearing
the national canvas —
this explosion of rock and jack pine
smattering texture

on blasted shield —
now we're getting sloppy
on diesel, on Molson.
These black and tan oils seep
into our pores,

the same ones
that dot this rock basin —
distorted reflections.
We rinse our faces
in lake water — the lapping
tongues of Pogamasing

growing louder, louder
still until sound
brushes steel branches —
and we reach for shards
of steel noise,
the fractured.

THE BRASH TIDES

I stripped the Atlantic bare,
gnashed my tail on Chignecto
rocks, your bearded cliffs

collapsing, the tufts
of fossil sands strewn
over water, strained

through baleen
lips, oh the exposed things,
they do not press

such sediments
forth, but back
up through mouthcombs,

the shy needles
etching initials
into the crags,

the rugged cheeks
of man dissolving,
the temper of breath.

There.

TRACING ONE WARM LINE

Through this bastard-child land, the boreal savage,
mammoth rock and birch, the leaves
like papier-mâché across this extended Shield —
this extended legend sleeved in highway
tunnels, barreling north and west, compass
be damned, we will not wait for Canada

in its adolescent search for identity — Canada,
your juvenile arc terranes do not mope for the savage,
the savant, the sage. They do not need a collective moral compass.
No, they are not the CBC. Yes, they are. Wavering leaves —
the deciduous, we drop to our knees on highway
carpet — the shagged rock, the Shield

a glassy scope, mirrored nimbus — the Shield
cut and tarred, a bevelled diamond. Face it, Canada,
you've got acne, you've got angst. It sprawls the highway,
seeps through newspaper and radio, those savage
beacons stuck in the mire of Trudeau give leave
to screens — we don't need a compass rose

to navigate these proverbial waters. Throw the compass
to the winds, the Chinooks blow kisses to your Eastern Shield.
Say hello to the Prairie mamas — leave
your apologies to the politicians. Canada,
get it together, man. Do your due diligence. You are not savage
and there is no residential school left to tame your highway

guilt. Buck up, darling. Grit your teeth, wind the highway.
For God's sake, I told you to lose the bloody compass.
And stop playing with your stick shift. Enough with the savage
comparisons below the border. This windshield
is not a two-way mirror, Canada,
so don't you scream superior at a reflection double-exposed, don't you
dare leave.

Well. You've been on your own for 151 years. I'll leave
you to your own devices, your chiselled highway
looks and provincial charm. Canada,
I love you but my compass
points south these days and I cannot shield
my eyes anymore — your savage

snowy tantrums are ugly like a CBC sitcom. Pass
the salt-n-vinegar chips — I'll keep watch, Canada, but my shield
is up, the crests of highways and leaves falling, the savage.

CALGARY, 1981

We hadn't settled
into the decade yet,
our collective browns
and oranges steeping gently
through duplex hallways —

tinged drapes and sunken tubs,
crinkled View-Master disks
and popcorn kernels
germinating deep within
crushed shag.

We were caught — up
in the foothills, corduroy
legs and cigarettes —
Prairie smoke,
a pregnant halo

circling us, nesting
in mustaches and duffle bags,
in Wayne Gretzky's trousers,
in kitchen whispers —
        formica formica formica

and decoder rings for left
hands.
        THIS IS IT.
        THIS ISN'T IT.

I was born under a big sky.

HITCHHIKERS

We travel in pairs,
prepare with rye
and woollen layers,
lay the base
for highway fictions,
these singsongs

lick the shoulders
of Quebec, smoke
the cigarettes of rocker moms
who drive Plymouth Dusters —
the ceiling droops

and we wait. For hours,
nothing but gravel,
rationed cheese sandwiches,
discussions of emergency
words — a signal
for escape.

We trundle down
bevelled highway
bundled in toggles,
yarned scarves and bags and bags,
perform an encore presentation
of *Fat Man Running Towards a Donut*

until we catch
Marvin's 18-wheeler
bound for Halifax,
toast this victory
with *fruits-des-champs*,
settle in for the haul.

But Marvin,
he'll get a little handsy,
so when you stage-whisper
            TIM THE TOOLMAN TAYLOR
I'll say I have to pee
on the side of the road

and we are out.
It is February and we are waiting,
emulsified with four o'clock
sun, down eastward bound,
laughing under green signs
pierced with white:
            St. Louis-du-Ha!-Ha!   *42 km*

LARRY BIRD MOWS THE LAWN

They gathered in droves,
knee socks and Converse
terry cloth shorts
the green and the white —
the broad *A*s,
raised diphthongs —
the locals
gathered in droves.

On sidewalks, on grey
and bubbled black, in cars —
lurching from half-opened windows,
snapping rolls of 24
in 35mm, in 110 —
those long pocket cameras,
flash eclipsed by sun
on sidewalks, on grey

focus. Bird's eyes
never waver from the task
at hand — palming
grips, delivering perfect
lines up and down
court green — clean
and courteous, but not without
focus. A bird's-eye

view of the win,
a postcard from Boston
with love to French Lick —
Indiana's self-professed
hick, six-foot-nine and pale
as the dickens — quiet
but not shy, a trash talker
from way back. When he thumbs
that aquiline nose at the ref, you know
the interview's off: the win.

MONTREAL POEM; OR, OUR HEARTS ARE NOT LIKE WHEELS; OR, LES HABITANTS

If I were to write
a Montreal poem,
or a poem about Montreal,

I would not mention
the mountain, or
Saint-Viateur, or
fire escape couture,
the Jew belle-lettrists,

the week we each ran into
Leonard Cohen,
buying plums at the depanneur,
or reclining on a bench
in Parc du Portugal.
Grey suits for everyone.

I would not ask
you to remember Jeanne-Mance
or Maisonneuve,
the parties

the parties,
the Labatt 50 and tequila,
late night promenades
in empty rooms with August windows.
Please, no slow dancing
in the street.

No sliding down lamp-
posts. No more
McGarrigles. No,
our hearts are not like wheels,
are they?

I would not say
this now, dear.
I would not start this poem again.

RIB

So she asks him why men chase women
and he does not answer, cocks
one eyebrow, pulls a carving knife from the drawer.

Lady,
it is not your heart I want
but the rib you stole.
Let me take what is mine.

He has always been a selfish lover.

MERCY FUCK

For you, David, I would
use my bare hands to
castrate the heavens
kiss the virile mess so when

you get there you will remember
our Halifax, how you stranded me in bloodstorms
under hemlock and pine, over words in the

darkness — gutted me with love,
abandoned my love, David, left me for the
vague blondes — they do not know how
I loved you, and now
David, not they, not even God, will bless you
                                        with a mercy fuck.

JOHN ISLAND I

There is a lot of plaid
in this kitchen.
It is October and we are arguing,
waxing over
the expiration date
of cream of tartar.
This label says 1992.
We are shutting down camp
before northern Ontario
becomes northern Ontario.

We were three
before you returned
in the crash-boat,
hair whipping your cheeks.
You brought Petit Tigre,
beer, and a vacuum pump.
We'll clean out the grease
traps tomorrow.

I'm getting better
at driving the old Belarus.
I worry only
when we cross the Kwai Bridge,
gargantuan tires navigating
wooden plank on plank,
and you, straddling the hitch
between tractor and trailer.

We map our claim
on Huron with names:
They paddled to *Mary's Cove*.
Meet me at *Chapel Point*.
Listen for the *Halfer*. For the *Fiver*.
No diving at the *Dive*.

We do dive, of course.
And Mary's pushing 70,
30 years on.
Last year her nephew married
on a southern farm. I was inside
the porta-john when it started
to shake. I heard Mary laugh.

TUЯBO

My friend Turbo is a son
of a bitch. My friend Turbo,
well — you might be wondering
about the name,
Turbo with a backwards *R*,
this backwoods cowboy

among the Ojibway
this beard a sign
of his whiteness
        it covers the white,
        sings out the white,
        the drowning of white —

skinned legends,
the shadows of birch-
papered boats
atop Huron's north
channel —

the mythology of Turbo
swims somewhere between
Blind River and Elliot Lake,
chokes on freshwater
silt and whisky,
the young guns smoking —
but stop.
Enough is enough.

So. Turbo.
He says it stands for
        TOUGH UGLY RUGGED BASTARD OUTDOORS
but you and I,
now, we know better
and this plaintive
man is not a man.

He is a boy, a cartoon-
watching figment
of 1980s mining town Ontario.
Oh, Turbo, you really
were the fastest junior racer
at *1-2-3-4 Ski Mount Dufour*
but you never could run fast
enough to outlive
your name.

A MAN I NEVER LOVED

Years ago I woke up in your bed, fully clothed
and reeling from our introduction the night before —
                                        not to mention the beer.
Sometime between 4 and 5 a.m., you took my arm
and confessed your death five years prior.
                                        You were 26 and I was 19.

You said I had lovely hair and two years left,
spoke of sex, pendulous breasts that belonged
        to women with exotic names like Soraja.
A rapport of repulsion and fascination,
ours spanned provinces, ignored borders.

When your parents moved to Sudbury, I was already there.
I spent my days answering telephones, nights drinking
your nickels away. After the bar closed, you and I
drove out to watch the slag, forgave each other's trespasses,
as we climbed fences, eschewed the signs,
                                        delighted in small crimes.

In Winnipeg you received word that your grandmother had died.
We smoked and talked of better times in the city,
your apartment on de l'Esplanade:
                                        red wine and maps.
You critiqued my taste in men, warned me of rogue
tree planters with outlandishly large dicks.

In a few years you will own property,
cook nutritious root vegetables for your wife
and daughter, whom I will meet in a noisy pub,
        strapped to your back in a modern papoose.
You will be a businessman on paternity leave.

But now, in Montreal again, it rains on Maisonneuve.
You gallantly offer to double me on your bicycle
across town. This is a balancing act, a feat

of strong thighs and hidden desire, pumping
all the way to the heart of the Plateau.
You are happy: a man
I never loved.

THE WHY AND THE HOW

Why are boats always women,
and where is Long Lake —
how you ride my mind

how to pet a dead horse
how to feed this hoop snake
and always why boats are women.

Why bathtubs crawl on fours,
and how water grows opaque
and still —you ride my mind:

run grey galleys worn and coarse,
teak and holly slats, the strakes.
If boats are always women

then men are the oars — slicing
pink for pink's sake:
you ride my mind

in circles. There is no shore
for us, only questions in the lake —
why boats are always women
and how you ride my mind.

GEOGRAPHY

Last night we slept without
covers, awoke in territories
marked with sheets, the curve
of your back, shadows and light.
At the border your hand grazes
my hip, forms a drawbridge.
This heat, gentle dictator
of such lines, lingers
heavy with your touch
and the space between.

JOHN ISLAND II

How many times
have we walked this beach?
And then, through pine
and brush sands, in darkness.
We don't carry flashlights.
A sign of weakness or hubris,
I don't know.

There were bears.
I'm still not sure
how you convinced
me to join the boys,
spreading honey and garbage
over the grease trap lids.
Perching on tractors,
blackened feet illuminated
in the bug-eyed lights of
July.

Now the canoes sleep,
the dining hall a quiet maze
of boats, sails strung
from steel knots.
Yesterday, we returned milk crates
after I lost the bet.

I called Farquhar's Dairy.
How to explain the presence
of 400 odd milk crates.
They sent a truck
to meet us on the other side.

It is October and we are moving
milk crates, stacking them like huge Legos,
first in the trailer, then
into the belly of the *Earl M.*
You insist on a photo:
wartime tugboat chock a block,
and me, wild-faced in 35mm
staring down the channel,
the rugged.

ON YONGE STREET

On Yonge Street it is Tuesday and I am unemployed,
but not without grace, basking in the afterglow
of last night's storm, today's ripe pickings.

Microcosm:
Papery women festooned with earrings, wigs
to fool themselves young. Mocha lattes
carried in the well-manicured hands of
corporate yogis. And babies, babies;
the stroller is not what it used to be;
and baby, even the babies are wearing designer scarves.

Earlier today, I stopped at the fruit stand
on the corner for some raspberries, cheaper
                                        than cherries and more useful.
The dill weed was on sale for 78 cents,
and Mr. Choi threw in a lemon for good measure.

Here I am, unemployed, out on the patio
with red sunglasses and a bucket of rain.

HIGHWAY 17

Oh you roared
through the border,
one hand planed through northern air,
the other kissing the wheel.
We navigate with waxed
egg salad and cassette tapes,
familiar graffiti:
            THIS IS INDIAN LAND.

Trespass through the Shield,
precambrian, the gutted rock
traversed by highway,
the paper birches
lurching unto the abandoned,
the bungalow motels and chipstands,
the summer Dairy Queen in Blind River.
So give'er.

Through Spragge
and Massey, this corridor
of tractors and boat trailers,
always one restaurant,
the one with the totem pole
out front, SERVING CHINESE AND CANADIAN FOOD,
closed since 1977 —
at least

we are getting used to two
lanes again. This is romance,
is memory, brush-fired
on rock, rusted
with smoke and slag,
the sons and daughters of Sudbury.

I will leave you
tonight in the Townehouse, soaking
in gin and whispers,
the dancing harpies of the nickel bin
        those who prey on our mined
        history of wood-panelled walls,
        the browns and the oranges,
        the Labatt 50, stubbed
        cigarettes in homemade
        ashtrays, felted glass
        on postage stamps,
        Pierre Trudeau in blackface.
        Just watch me —

AULD LANG SYNE, ETC.

In Montreal you ran shirtless and sweating,
over the mountain — under a cross,
the city's proverbial eye in the sky —
it was summer and you had been drinking,
escaping the home and garden police of Westmount,
                    high-pressure systems swelling, engorged —

a shared troposphere, the anticyclone of designer tiles
and kitchens, business trips and $9 loaves of bread — the organic
zeal of a woman in her forties. She's got books on the bedside,
                    texts on polyamory and it's freaking you out.
You went vegetarian, yes, but shared interests are not a pre-req

for marriage — at least, this is what you say
over dinner in Toronto. We won't hold back
and you never have — tonight you delight me with isms
(I can't let you get away) with. Has it been seven years?
I like your beard.

You remember the slag and I don't remember your car,
an old Nissan Stanza in gunmetal — but poetry is dead
and you can't smoke in the Townehouse anymore.

You once told me the most beautiful things
you'd ever seen were two hippie girls dancing
in the rain downtown on a McGill lawn,
                    breasts soaked in the gentle tropics of September
(but that was before you had children).

So gimme a lovepunch —
drunk on papadums and beer, gin and tonics
at a dive on Bloor Street in winter, in the stretch
between Christmas and New Year's — your trip
to Cancun with your wife looms, childless (I am) —

for the first time in so many years.
                    You are 42 and I am 35.
I won't ask if you are happy.

EULOGY

"Shed no tears!" — Stan Rogers

He favoured turtlenecks
and his baldness lent him years
decanted through song,
the sediments of working men
and women, floating

through such shanties made
modern — the plaid fists
pounding on pine
in Maritime kitchens —
the lace and rye-

soaked beards of 1983
are back in fashion.
Halifax, you and I
will not forget.
We could cry the harbour,

float the Citadel,
but why disturb the captain
while he slumbers heavy in the tape deck.

IN SECHELT

Sechelt seashells bathe the sea shore.

See shells, see shells, buy the sea shore.

See Chelle tease 'ells b'y! Sheesh! Or

See Chelle's seashells by the she-shore.

She shells she-shells! Buy the sea's whore!

Sea's hell, sea's hell, boys: these sea sores.

Cease, Chelle. Cease, Chelle. Buoy the she-shore.

She sells seashells by the sea shore.

YUKON RIVER

We paddle nights,
carve jays in beryl
waters, the salmon lustre
cast of a generous latitude,
the forgiving morning.
We have our routines.

You will fry granola
mid-current, rest
the teetery stove
between calves,
browned —

sugar the pan,
enameled with buttery
soap and pinecone
flecks, the filmy
ashes of late

night chats with Germans,
the singing Germans,
those who wave
from rock beds —
Oh girls, see you
tomorrow night, girls,
see you —

under tarps, thunder
heads, the massive,
the stone faces looming
upon grey slumber,
these Klondike graves —

wooden cribs,
muted. In the tent,
I will place a knife
between us to hold
off the dark.

MR. PEANUT

Consider Mr. Peanut
Consider his refined taste
Consider your refined taste for even considering
the refined taste of the most refined of all legumes
Consider that monocle, that top hat
The cane, and those darling spats
Consider those darling spats

Consider the scandals, darling
Consider the headlines
Mr. Peanut is not a nut
    is a legume
    is your mother
    is my father
    is a fiscal conservative
    is a social liberal
    did not vote for Jimmy Carter
    was a regular at Studio 54
    when he wasn't sunning his shell at Martha's
    Vineyard, that is
    is engaged to the Sun-Maid raisin lady
    left her at the alter
    is a homo
    is a dandy
    is more flexible than you think
    declines to comment
    wrote the book of love
    has faith in God above
    if the Bible tells him so
    is a zealot
    is a scientologist
    is a Mormon
    is a Southern Baptist
    is John Lennon
    is a poster boy
    is a prefect

is a headmaster
is a cane
a monocle
a hat
and those darling spats
Rat-a-tat-tat

Is Mr. Peanut more American, or less American, than you?
Is Mr. Peanut more refined, or less refined, than you?
Is Mr. Peanut more than, or less than, you?
Is Mr. Peanut more or less you?
Is Mr. Peanut more or less
Is he more
Less

SHARP FLESH

Do not be fooled by this, his soft eyes,
his beard, auburn tufts
that betray darker locks, limbs.
His shoulders, warm with laughter,
strong with weights: dead and alive,
the raw exercise of memory.
His hands do not give away his profession,
but lend themselves to calloused dignity,
ink and algae.
Do not touch them.

He is so sharp.
He is so sharp, ladies, and he will cut you with his flesh.

TAXIDERMY

"Cupid, draw back your bow and let your arrow go
straight to my lover's heart for me."
— Sam Cooke

What to do.
What to do with this mess:
his carcass, veined
leather and whisky
blood —

first to gut
the radio, then
to place the hand —
                    just so.
Slide the index
finger broadside
the arrow

brace and pull
                    and pull,
the damned pulp
will follow,
the egregious
mass —

the poor used thing.
Hollow it.
Scrape the flesh
under your nails
and tear

down his Jericho
walls — the four
rooms where you lay
now one,

empty but for sound —
echoes of rhythm
and blues left
to undulate,
not to cease

but to repeat,
stitched within dead
tissue and sold
to whomever.

ORGAN DONOR

I carry you now: against
the dark: your pulp

pumps against
my thigh, a red

fist of pulp: stop.

The corpuscles, they
leak stigma, dye

the inner linens,
folded. Now I fold:

you into my satchel,
cannot tell you

can never give you
can never look you in the

artery of the New York
subway: tangled veins

siphon me
to you: the blood

source of shrapnel:
shards of rosy glass

capillaries: artisan.

I REMEMBER THE WORDS

But not the tune.
If I grow sentimental, dear.
If I grow black, if I glow blue.
If I go back.
Forgive me.

If I write of you, now, as then.
If I think of you.
If I have kept our score,
                    and more,
let me keep

you,
my bearded one,
my Old Fashioned,
all sugars and bitters.

The jukebox is broken.
The bar is closed.
The lights, they move,
they flicker,
              outside and in,
they flicker.

And I will call Nova Scotia
power. I will use a rotary
phone. They will send a man.
He will fix everything.

I will gather rations.
I will hold the torch close.
I will keep my radio on.
But the Righteous Brothers are dead.
And they cannot sing.
And there's no Rockaday Johnny,
with his *ooh-eee, ooh-ee*

our loves a-gonna grow and grow, oh wild one.
Swan songs.

Oh my love, my darling.
Oh my love.
Oh my.
Oh.

CARPENTRY

These days I dream of carpenters and their sons.
Wood is not absolute. I am.
Straddle is an unfair word, a resolute action.
There were three beds.

Brown pay telephones. A gray scarf.
These things only serve to dilute.
A warm house will make you forget.
                                                            He did.
Resilience is the kindest punishment.

SUDBURY, ONT.

We will not sleep.

Tonight we boulder rocks for a bird's-eye
view of the General Hospital, hiking nimbly
through the woods, our steps recorded
on well-worn footpaths. Look, why don't you.
I want you to see the wooden ladder on the
third birch tree. It belongs to my father and his brothers.
Scrape your knee on the same rock that cut my sister
at four, her legs red and white to match her dress.

Because we are here tonight I will let you
tell me about your awkward years,
past initials carved into rock, further preserved
in a photograph taken by a current boyfriend,
amused by this northern graffiti. Let's run
up the stairs to Alexander P.S., sip
vodka before homeroom, spend the morning
crying in the principal's office, promise
never to drink again.

But here we are with wine and beer,
perspective. When your boyfriend
emerges from a boozy nap, you will
depart with midnight hot dogs and
I will be left alone with Sudbury,
to swim in Long Lake,

to wave frantically at my mother in the paddleboat
as she lights a cigarette, pedals away from
my brother, wet with clown eyelashes and tears

to remember for Emily and for Steve,
            for small boys with hammers and funny faces,
            for little girls, all knees and freckles, melting
            for grown men who do not live on McNaughton Street.

GRACE ESCAPES

I. ST. ANDREW'S CHURCH BASEMENT

After Sunday school
the boys roughhouse,
get their ya-yas out,
skidding on linoleum
squares, all striped
shirts, PF flyers.
And oh look,
there's Peter Block
and Billy too —
the boys of Patterson Street —
an innocent circle
jerk of whirled noogies,
cops and robbers,
you know the drill.
(Well it was all fun
and games anyway,
until someone dropped
the piano
on my father.)

II. BOYS WILL BE BOYS

A seven-year-old version
of my father throws an axe
over the roof — the damned
hatchet lodges neatly into
Billy's head.
(He'll live to tell the tale.)

III. THE JOKERMAN IS GONE

My father can't play Scrabble by himself, or tennis.
He can't call anyone to jaw about Jack the Bear
or Martina's forehand. No one else owns two copies
of Bob Dylan's *Infidels*. There is no record player.
There is no brother.
(Half a century later, the axe falls through.)

GERMANS LOVE DAVID HASSELHOFF

All Germans love David Hasselhoff
but not all Germans love David Hasselhoff equally.
Contrary to pop-lore, David Hasselhoff
did not bring down the Berlin Wall alone.
Enter the light-up jacket. Enter the hair.
Forget about the Speedo, folks.
Germans love David Hasselhoff as David
Hasselhoff, the man behind the anthem.
In 1989, "Looking for Freedom" soared east and west; the
jam was hot and so were the stereos. East Berliners just wanted to
kick out the jams — David Hasselhoff's jams —
liberation by boombox.
Michael Jackson had nothing on David Hasselhoff's
New Year's at the Wall. Enter the light-up jacket. Enter the hair.
Oh, I've been looking for freedom. I've been looking so long. Oh,
please, David Hasselhoff. Piano key scarf? Really, David Hasselhoff?
Quit now while you are ahead, David Hasselhoff — your lyrics,
rote in teenage minds, in middle-aged relief, will not
sing softly into the next century,
though we will not forget the light-up jacket. The hair.
Up the ante, David Hasselhoff. Rent a
Volkswagen, David Hasselhoff, and drive all the
way to 2018, David Hasselhoff. After the crash, the Germans will
x-ray you, illuminate your insides — no bones, just
you and your YouTube cheeseburger, the outline of a cock, *die*
zirkumzision.

BLOND SATAN

What a lot of you don't know
is that Sam Spade was really
a very good tennis player
and a member of the Palisades
Club and everything.
He had quite the forehand,
but you know,
it was his backhand
that made the ladies cry.

BOUND

To bind the feet, to fold the sole.
To use the hand to break the foot,
miniscule fractures that creak,

crinkle exquisitely. Snap the bone
to sculpt the hoof, delicate and hideous.
These bandages are torture devices,

pulled taut, tighter and tighter still,
until a cleft is carved between
heel and sole. Curate the stench

of indention, indentured sex.
Three inches to stand on,
to wedge into dainty slippers.

Stare at the woman, bound
to three inches, to stumps
of beauty long abandoned.

ICE PICK LOBOTOMY

They practised
on grapefruits, peeled
back navels
like eyelids

stamped *X* deep
into the sockets,
the dilated veins
exposed,

wielded rubber
mallets to test
the reflexes of ice
picks,

against the thin.
Who would puncture
such blood matter
7 cm

within, scrambling
sacs of citrus
lobe upon
lobe,

scraping
the soupy cavities
to make room
for what.

BECAUSE

Because the Atlantic.
Because the Pacific.
Because the hemispheres.
Because the equator, the belted
    cinching of guts, the green and the blue.
Because the guts.
Because the flaws.
Because we are heavy.
Because we are raw.
Because my mother has nerves.
Because my father shaved his mustache in 1981. And 1983. 1987.
Because his father wrote with his left hand.
Because Zuma rains.
Because lobsters shriek.
Because old men play cribbage in undershirts.
Because birches peel.
Because dogs know.
Because lakes smoke.
Because that teacher told me to mouth the words.
Because there are indoor voices and outdoor voices.
Because there are indoor shoes and outdoor shoes
    and no shoes at all.
Because because.
Because there are hands.
Because we carve our names in desks.
Because we carve our names in stone.
Because we are not permanent.
Because we look at the sun.
Because we singe our eyes.
Because there are eyes,
the scratched inky things,
the sanding of iris,
the sleep of because.

BARBER

First the haircut
levers the chair so he may look you in the eye
asks you of your wife did you catch the game these goddamn potholes
circles his prey, slowly with rapid snips and backslaps
He has his methods

Then the shave
submit to the cold lather
his hand, damp and strong around your neck
his breath: menthol cigarettes and gouda
and the blade, his too. A tiny mirror
reflecting mercy with every cough,
every flick of the wrist

WISDOM TEETH

Tonight you will rest,
jaw stuffed with cotton, bloody
with welcome cavities, fresh
wounds, remnants of an otherwise
peaceful nap earlier this afternoon
in the Victoria General.

Tomorrow he will telephone,
with remorse and without love,
prematurely rip each stitch, leave you
to drain. There, there; there
is no time to dissolve, dear.
The ambulance is here.

Your chart will hang off the bed,
display name, age, sex: details
he will choose to forget. Remember,
you are a textbook case.
It is not often that oral surgeries lead to cardiac arrest.

BRIDE AND WOLF

"A bride without a head, a wolf without a foot." — Moonstruck

Pour yourself a scotch and listen to the man, wounded
by his own and now left with one good hand,
one wooden reminder to rub his wrist: this friction,
heat combined with the clicking and clacking,
the sound of knife and carcass, bloody. To feed
his blood, she says, and wrings her hands,
wipes her apron. The table divides them,
gives space for his lupine arms and legs
stretched below, leaves room for invitation,
accusation: seven years condensed, neat.

Earlier in the bakery how could she know
when he asked her to bring him the big knife,
how could she know this lunatic, Ronny,
and his touch, shoulders and wood.
Opera in the kitchen,
straight through till morning.

ORCA FART

"My life is a work of art." — J.

I think of you when I think of Saint-Laurent —
fair artery of our city, always
with the buttery drunks lurching
in, lurching out of the Copacabana,
the Bifteck — or Miami, the upstairs dive.

That night we drank until 3 a.m.
at Le Swimming. I remember, James.
I remember those barstools, how I fell
close when you leaned in to tell
me that your armpits smelled like vaginas.
Vaginas, James.

Can you blame me for dancing away
from your belt buckle,
your rogue arms — I didn't know
then, James, what I know now.
How this would not be the last of your epigraphs.

How I would sit here seven cities later
eating cereal and thinking of your vaginas.

CONDUCTOR

This woman owns the room,
five foot seven and leggy, darling.
Drink her in, all blonde and lipsticked,
that voice

and those red lacquered nails, hands
that conduct electricity with every
sudden move. Orchestral light.

JUST GRIT

Roofs in Montreal beg to be conquered,
always with those rickety black wrought iron
ladders spiraling up to God
or at least the electric Jesus

Bringing anyone here is risky —
I wore a skirt and you held the ladder
We had the city in our hands
and we gave it up for the kitchen counter

I told you these roofs in Montreal are graveyards,
final resting grounds for empty bottles of Labatt 50
No flowers, just grit and one last night

THE FREE

We are the orange   the lit
benches cheap beer
swilling river

free (the Hudson)   free
(the ferry)   free (we
the   people)

We the Manhattanese
our designer jeans
our glasses! and stiletto Nikes
our   assless chaps!

chapped in wind
and   water
flame

(the ricochet of   free)
the lichened copper
and the   spiked
tiara   the colossal

feet   the fallen
arches the   same
as (ours)

ON THE DERBY DAY

In Kentucky we drink roses,
prick our tongues, swallow
five hundred and fifty-four times.

We came here to see
about a dead horse. Still,
I wore organdy, if only

because you insisted on
that seersucker suit, cufflinks
glinting with wet heat

underneath, bauble
on bauble: metal meets wrist,
distinct bone and hairline.

Ours is a private box, natch.
We don't do well with others,
never have. Too occupied

with beards and curls,
and dozens of neuroses,
braided. One year ago,

you leapt onto the table,
serenaded me with bourbon,
stuffed julep leaves into the silks

of your pocket. Your chest bled mint,
bled mine. My ear pressed
against your heaving heart,

my hands groped the knots
of your shoulders, knees.
And this was not enough

to keep you. When the gate
broke open, your chest
thundered, all sinew

and ropes, exploding,
ripping your shirt,
slicing new love

lines into my hands. Big horse,
you are gone and I am left
to clutch the blue

and the white you wore.
To smell the leather
of your bootstraps,

the liquored declarations:
you're my only
and I'm your only,

but. Big horse, you
ran.

THE LOAD OUT / STAY

It wasn't a date — but,
you bought the beer
walked slow on April sidewalks
told me your last girlfriend was a nightmare
to shop with — we passed an abandoned factory
and I heard Jackson Browne crooning —
1978, 1978, 1978
dissolving in grey and in blue,
in the tongues of California freeways
so far ahead —
I wonder: will we get there?

FOR BORIS

Goddamn! Your Datsun was a beast of a car
not even fit for Highway 17, let alone the 400
Madness at ninety miles per hour
            kilometres are for women and children

Wind sheared the rear-view mirror right off
but you and I knew better, and even we
are capable of performing back alley surgery,
            duct tape and whiskey never fail

At the border you stepped out for a coffee
and I suppose I should have declared you
Rest assured, neither of us sat comfortably after that,
            customs officials do not flinch at anything

Boris! Consider this my final apology
Now I dream gently of ice blocks and you

INFLUENCE

I fear that I channel a certain
combination of Ondaatje and a vacation
pamphlet for Canada. Am I so obvious?
Well, I'm listening to too much Fleetwood Mac,
anyway. I'm not smoking and it's not analog,
but here at 2 a.m., it is always 1979 —
Buckingham and Nicks caught in a freeze frame
mid-song, accusations and affairs be damned,
his arm around her waist. There are two
sets of lips. There is one microphone.
I want to fill in this space between mouth and mouth
because they are our mouths
and this is my microphone
and there is so much to say.

ACKNOWLEDGEMENTS

Many of these poems originally appeared in the following publications: *carte blanche*, *CV2*, *The Dalhousie Review*, *Event*, *Existere*, *The Fiddlehead*, *Grain*, *Hart House Review*, *The Malahat Review*, *Riddle Fence*, and *Washington Square Review*.

Thank you to Michael Holmes and the ECW Press team. To David Lehman and others at The New School for their attention to this collection in its earliest days. Special thanks to Brookes Moody, whose advice, friendship, and insight proved invaluable in the creation of this book. Cue the Van Morrison.

Much grace to my family, especially to my sister Pamela for her constant encouragement and support. To Montreal and New York and Sudbury and Toronto. To John Island.

In memory of George Grace — editor, sports writer, music enthusiast, Y's man, collector of records and records, of which there is none whicher than.